Improve your aural! Grade 2

Paul Harris and John Lenehan

Contents

fabermusic.com

© 2006 by Faber Music Ltd
First published in 2006 by Faber Music Ltd
Bloomsbury House 74–77 Great Russell Street London WC1B 3DA
Music processed by Music Set 2000
Design by Susan Clarke
Printed in England by Caligraving Ltd
All rights reserved
ISBN10: 0-571-52456-7
EAN13: 978-0-571-52456-3

CD recorded in Rectory Studio, High Wycombe, March 2006
Created and produced by John Lenehan
Thanks to Godstowe School Chamber Choir 2006 and Laurel Hopkinson
℗ 2006 Faber Music Ltd
© 2006 Faber Music Ltd

Why is aural important?

You may wonder why you have to do aural at all. The answer is, that aural will really help you improve as a musician. And this may surprise you – it will help perhaps more than *any other* single musical skill.

Aural is all about understanding and processing music that you hear and see, in your head. By doing so, you will find that your own playing improves enormously. You will be able to play more expressively and stylistically, be more sensitive to quality and control of tone, your music reading will improve, you will be able to spot your own mistakes, be more sensitive to others when playing or singing in an ensemble, be more aware of intonation, improve your ability to memorise music and improve your ability to improvise and compose.

All the many elements of musical training are of course connected. So, when working through the activities in this book you will be connecting with many of them. You'll be listening, singing, clapping, playing your instrument, writing music down, improvising and composing – as well as developing that vital ability to do well at the aural tests in your grade exams!

Aural is not an occasional optional extra – just to be taken off a dusty shelf a few days (or even hours) before a music exam. It's something you can be developing and thinking about all the time. And as you go through the enjoyable and fun activities in these books you'll realise how important and useful having a good musical ear (being good at aural) really is.

How to use this book

When you have a few minutes to spare (perhaps at the beginning or end of a practice session), sit down with your instrument, by your CD player, and open this book. Choose a section and then work through the activities – you needn't do much each time. But whatever you do, do it carefully, repeating any activity if you feel it will help. In fact many of the activities will be fun to do again and again. And make sure that you come back to the book on a regular basis.

So, good luck and enjoy improving your aural skills!

Paul Harris and John Lenehan

For U.S. readers:

Bar	= Measure
Upbeat	= Pick-up
Semitone	= Half step
Note	= Tone

Section 1 Pulse

By now, you will have met music that has either two or three beats in a bar. The number of beats in the bar can also give music character. Match the following by drawing a line to connect the correct pairs:

track
2 On this track you'll hear a waltz and a march. Which is which?

Piece 1 _____

Piece 2 _____

Listen to the track again and this time clap the pulse and count the beats out loud.

track
3 Some of the examples you'll hear in Grade 2 will be in *compound time*. This means that each beat is divided into three instead of two (which is called *simple time*). The pieces on track 3 are examples of music in compound time. Listen carefully to how each beat is divided into three.

Some pieces begin with an 'upbeat' (or *anacrucis*, which comes from the Greek meaning 'prelude'. In the U.S. it is often called a 'pick-up'). We use upbeats a lot in speech. Here are some words where the first syllable is like an upbeat in music. Say them out loud:

sonata Madonna piano potato recorder awake trombone

listening activities

track 4

1 This track has four examples of Christmas carols, all beginning with an upbeat. Count the beats out loud, beginning with 'one' *after* the upbeat. How many beats are there in each bar? It will be either 2 or 3.

1 _____   3 _____

2 _____   4 _____

track 5

2 Listen to the five pieces by Mozart on this track. Some of them begin with an upbeat and some on the first beat of the bar – the 'downbeat'. You'll hear each just once. Write down whether they begin with an upbeat (U) or on the downbeat (D).

1 _____   4 _____

2 _____   5 _____

3 _____

track 6

3 Here's an exercise to help you develop your own inner metronome. You'll hear three bars of a pulse in 2-time with counting, and then it will stop. Continue counting on your own and silently in your head. In which bar and on which beat does the sound occur? What is the sound?

track 7

4 Here's a similar example in 3-time. In which bar and on which beat does the sound occur? This time the sound is played by an instrument. Can you tell which one?

track 8

5 Some of the pieces on this track are in simple time and some in compound time. You'll hear each piece once. Write down S (Simple time) or C (Compound time) after each piece.

1 _____   4 _____

2 _____   5 _____

3 _____   6 _____

6 Here are four pieces of music in 2-time. Clap (or tap) the pulse and join in as soon as you can.

7 Here are four pieces in 3-time. Again, clap (or tap) the pulse and join in as soon as you can.

8 The examples on this track will be either in 2-time or 3-time. Clap or tap the pulse of each of the musical excerpts, joining in as soon as you can. After each one, write down whether it was in two or three.

1 _____   2 _____   3 _____   4 _____   5 _____

9 In this exercise you'll hear a series of short rhythmic phrases in 2-time over a steady pulse. Clap or tap back exactly the rhythm that you hear like an echo. The first example is done for you.

10 Here are some more similar exercises, now in 3-time. Clap or tap back the exact rhythm.

11 This time, instead of repeating the rhythm, improvise your own rhythmic answer to each rhythm.

12 Listen to the phrase on this track, which will be repeated four times. Write down the rhythm on the line below:

$$\|\ \frac{2}{4} \ \rule{5cm}{0.4pt} \ | \ \rule{5cm}{0.4pt} \ \|$$

13 Now here's a phrase in 3-time, which will be repeated four times. Write down the rhythm on the line below:

$$\|\ \frac{3}{4} \ \rule{5cm}{0.4pt} \ | \ \rule{5cm}{0.4pt} \ \|$$

14 Ask your teacher to play you one of the pieces you are learning. Clap or tap the pulse. How many beats are there in the bar?

15 Using a piece you are currently working on, try to hear the first four bars in your head. Still without the music, have a go at answering the following questions:

● How many beats are there in each bar? _____

● Does the piece have an upbeat? _____

● Is it in simple or compound time? _____

● What are the time values of the first two notes of the tune?

  _____

● Are there any rests in the first four bars? _____

● If so, what are they? _____

● Hear the first four bars in your head and at the same time tap the pulse.

● Now hear the pulse in your head and tap the rhythm.

● Write down the rhythm of the melody of the first four bars. Put in the time signature:

‖————————————|————————————|————————————|————————————‖

Come back and repeat this exercise using other pieces or using other four-bar phrases from the same piece.

Section 2   Pitch

On your instrument, play the first five notes of any major scale – choose one that is comfortably in your singing register. Now sing those notes, firstly to *lah*, then to the numbers 1 – 2 – 3 – 4 – 5. Now sing 5 – 4 – 3 – 2 – 1.

Now sing the following patterns. Play the first note (any comfortable note) on the piano or on your instrument, then sing the pattern and then play it to hear whether you were accurate.

1   1 – 2 – 3 – 2 – 1

2   1 – 2 – 3 – 4 – 3

3   1 – 2 – 3 – 5 – 3   4.

 4   1 – 3 – 5 – 3 – 1   What is this pattern part of?

Here is the first shape from the previous activity written out in C major. Write out the others in the same way:

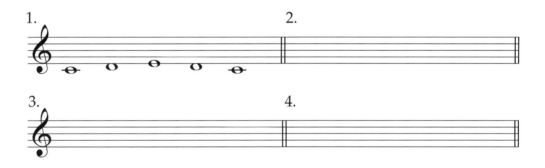

Now look at each phrase and hear it in your head. Then sing each phrase reading the music.

listening activities

track 17

1 You'll hear some five-note phrases on this track. Write them down using numbers. The first one is done for you.

1   1 – 2 – 3 – 2 – 1

2 _____   **4** _____

3 _____   **5** _____

track 18

2 Listen to each phrase and sing back exactly what you hear. The first phrase is sung back as an example.

track 19

3 After a four-bar introduction, you'll hear a series of five-note phrases over an accompaniment. After each, improvise your own answering phrase. The first one is done for you as an example.

track 20

4 Here are some phrases for you to sing back like an echo. Sing your responses as soon as you've heard the piano play the phrase. The first one is done for you.

track 21

5 Here are some more phrases for you to sing back like an echo. Sing your responses as soon as you've heard the piano play the phrase.

track 22

6 Sometimes you'll hear notes in octaves higher or lower than your singing range. Don't try to sing them at pitch, but at your usual, natural and comfortable octave. After you hear each note on this track, try to sing it at your own comfortable pitch. The first one is done for you.

track 23

7 You've probably been singing most of the previous exercises smoothly (or *legato*), but part of the fun of aural tests is singing the phrases back with character as well as the correct notes. In the next group of exercises, try to sing back what you hear as accurately as you can – with all the details. Some examples are played at unusual octaves – sing them back at your usual, natural and comfortable octave.

track 24

8 Here are some examples similar to those you'll get in an exam.

Section 3 # Hearing changes

For Grade 2 you will have to say whether the change in a phrase is rhythmic or melodic. The next few exercises are to help you hear melodic changes. A melodic change means that a note has been altered to a new one, either higher or lower than the original.

listening activities

1 Each of the ten four-note phrases you'll hear will be followed by the same phrase with one note changed. Write down whether the note that has been changed is higher (H) or lower (L) than in the first playing.

1 _____   2 _____   3 _____   4 _____   5 _____

6 _____   7 _____   8 _____   9 _____   10 _____

2 This time write down which number note was changed (1, 2, 3 or 4).

1 _____   2 _____   3 _____   4 _____   5 _____

6 _____   7 _____   8 _____   9 _____   10 _____

3 Now you'll hear some two-bar phrases in 3-time played twice with a melodic change in either the first or second bar. Write down in which bar the change occurred.

1 _____   2 _____   3 _____   4 _____   5 _____

6 _____   7 _____   8 _____   9 _____   10 _____

4 This time write down whether the changed note was higher (H) or lower (L).

1 _____   2 _____   3 _____   4 _____   5 _____

6 _____   7 _____   8 _____   9 _____   10 _____

5 Now you'll hear ten more examples. Write down in which bar the change occurred (1 or 2) and whether the changed note was higher (H) or lower (L). The first example is answered for you.

1 _2_ _H_   2 __ __   3 __ __   4 __ __   5 __ __

6 __ __   7 __ __   8 __ __   9 __ __   10 __ __

6 Now you'll hear either a rhythmic or melodic change. So you'll have to think fast! First of all write down whether it's a rhythmic change (R) or a melodic change (M). Then whether the change was in bar 1 or 2. If it was a rhythmic change, describe the change as best you can and if it was a melodic change, say whether the changed note was higher or lower. The first one is done for you.

track 75
track 76
track 77
track 78
track 79
track 80

Change	Bar	Description
_R_	_1_	_The first note was longer_
__	__	_____
__	__	_____
__	__	_____
__	__	_____
__	__	_____

7 Make up your own pair of phrases – with a melodic or rhythmic change in the second phrase. Write it down and play it to a friend or your teacher. Can they spot the difference?

8 Choose a passage from a piece you are currently learning and make some changes in the rhythm or melody. Play the passage to your teacher and see whether he or she can spot the differences.

Learning to listen to music

The new feature in Grade 2 is tempo (speed) changes. There will either be a *rallentando* (getting slower) or an *accelerando* (getting faster).

listening activities

track
(81)

1 Listen to these examples and then write down whether the phrase ended with a *rallentando* (*rall.*) or an *accelerando* (*accel.*)

1 _____   **4** _____

2 _____   **5** _____

3 _____

track
(82)

2 This time the *rall.* or *accel.* will be combined with a *crescendo* or *diminuendo*. After hearing each phrase, write down whether there was a *rall.* or *accel.* at the end and whether it was accompanied by a *crescendo* (*cresc.*) or *diminuendo* (*dim.*). The first one is done for you.

1 *Rall./Cresc.*   **4** _____

2 _____   **5** _____

3 _____

3 Each of these tracks comprises a piece that combines all these features with those you studied in Grade 1. Each piece will be played twice and then you will be asked to answer two questions:

    1 Where was the quietest part of the music?

    2 Did the tempo change as the music became quieter at the end?

    3 In the loud section, were the notes smooth or detached?

    4 Did the tempo stay the same in the middle section?

    5 Were the changes from quiet to loud sudden or gradual?

track **83**

track **84**

track **85**

_____   _____

_____   _____

_____   _____

4 This time you'll hear each piece only once before having to answer the questions:

    1 Was the first section quieter than the second?

    2 Was the change from loud to quiet sudden or gradual?

    3 Did the tempo change anywhere?

    4 Which sections had detached notes?

    5 Did the tempo stay the same in the smooth section?

track **86**

track **87**

track **88**

_____   _____

_____   _____

_____   _____

5 Using a piece you are currently working on, try the following:

- Add a *rall.* and *accel.* (in pencil) and perform the piece to your teacher. Can your teacher spot where these changes of tempo occur?

- Where is the loudest part of the piece?

- Where is the quietest part of the piece?

- Play the piece ignoring all the markings!

- Play the piece really exaggerating all the markings!

- Play the piece reversing all the dynamic markings (e.g. $\boldsymbol{p} = \boldsymbol{f}$, *cresc.* = *dim.* etc.)

- Play the smooth sections *staccato* and the detached sections smoothly or, if the piece is mostly smooth, play it *staccato* and if it's mostly detached, play it all smoothly.

- Play the piece as expressively as possible, making the most of all the markings.

Section 5 # Making connections

These fun activities show you how aural connects with all the other aspects of music. Choose one or two each time you practise.

... with intervals

Play a note and then, in your head, hear the note a semitone above (for example, play C and then hear C♯). Sing the note and then play it to see how accurate you were. Can you find any semitones in the pieces you are currently studying?

... with scales

Play the first note of a minor scale you know well and then hear that note in your head. Now play the scale very slowly, pre-hearing each note in your head before you play it.

... with tone quality

Play the scale you chose for the above exercise again – this time listening to the quality of every note as you play it. Are all notes really matched in quality and quantity (dynamic level)?

... with sight-reading

Choose a sight-reading piece* and try to hear it first in your head. Then play it.

... with memory

Find a four-bar phrase from a piece you are learning. Play it a few times, then, without the music, hear it in your head and then play it from memory.

... with instruments

Listen to this track and then connect the boxes:

clarinet	played 1st
violin	played 2nd
trombone	played 3rd
organ	played 4th

* For example from *Improve your sight-reading!* Grade 2

... with music history

As a developing musician you will need to recognise the changing historical styles of music. Understanding style and musical periods will also help you to play your pieces with more conviction and authority.

Here are the names of the four main musical periods with typical combinations of instruments. Read them carefully. On the track you'll hear eight different musical examples. Using the information in the boxes, decide which period each comes from, and join the boxes.

Baroque music is often bright and celebratory
- harpsichord
- strings, trumpets and drums

Classical music is elegant and balanced
- piano
- wind octet

Romantic music is often rich and emotional
- piano and orchestra
- piano

20th/21st century music can do anything
- jazz band
- unusual combinations of instruments

piece 1

piece 2

piece 3

piece 4

piece 5

piece 6

piece 7

piece 8

A final message from the authors!

Answers

(by CD track number)

Section 1: *Pulse*

2 Waltz, then March

4 1: 3, 2: 2, 3: 3, 4: 2

5 1: D, 2: U, 3: U, 4: D, 5: U

6 Bar 13, first beat – whistle

7 Bar 10, second beat – guitar

8 1: C, 2: S, 3: S, 4: C, 5: S, 6: S

11 1: 2, 2: 3, 3: 2, 4: 3, 5: 2

15

16

Section 2: *Pitch*

17 2: 1, 2, 3, 4, 3   3: 1, 2, 3, 5, 3
      4: 1, 3, 2, 3, 1   5: 1, 3, 5, 3, 1

Section 3: *Hearing changes*

25–34 1: H, 2: L, 3: L, 4: H, 5: L, 6: L, 7: H, 8: L, 9: H, 10: L

35–44 1: 4, 2: 3, 3: 1, 4: 2, 5: 2, 6: 1, 7: 2, 8: 4, 9: 3, 10: 4

45–54 1: 2, 2: 1, 3: 2, 4: 1, 5: 1, 6: 2, 7: 2, 8: 1, 9: 1, 10: 2

55–64 1: L, 2: L, 3: H, 4: H, 5: L, 6: H , 7: H, 8: L, 9: H, 10: L

66–74 2: 1/L, 3: 1/L, 4: 1/H, 5: 2/H, 6: 2/L, 7: 1/L, 8: 1/H,
      9: 2/H, 10: 2/L

76 M/1 – the fourth note was higher

77 M/2 – the last note was higher

78 R/2 – the first note of the second bar was longer (dotted)

79 M/1 – the third note was lower

80 R/1 – the first note was shorter

Section 4: *Learning to listen to music*

81 1: *accel.* 2: *rall.* 3: *rall.* 4: *accel.* 5: *rall.*

82 2: *accel./cresc.* 3: *accel./dim.* 4: *rall./dim.* 5: *rall./cresc.*

83 End / sudden

84 Yes (*rall.*) / detached

85 No (slower) / sudden

86 No / sections 1 and 3

87 Yes / sudden

88 Sudden / no (*rall.*)

Section 5: *Making connections*

89 Trombone, clarinet, violin, organ

90 Baroque – 2 & 8, Classical – 1 & 6,
      Romantic – 3 & 5, 20th/21st century – 4 & 7